I stood outside myself
asleep, awake and aware
in the catch
of yesterday's breeze
and the shimmer
of destined dreams.

~ **Candice James**
(excerpt pg. 31)

Also by Candice James

Print Books

Transitioning
10 PAKs –4; 3; 2; and 1
A Potpourri of Paintings;
The Still Small Voice of Soul;
Spiritual Whispers; Atmospheres;
Blue Silence; Call of the Crow;
Imagination's Reverie; Short Shots 2;
The Depth of the Dance;
Behind the One-Way Mirror;
The Path of Loneliness
Rithimus Aeternam; The Water Poems;
Short Shots; City of Dreams;
Merging Dimensions; The 13th Cusp;
Colors of India; Purple Haze;
A Silence of Echoes; Shorelines; Ekphrasticism;
Midnight Embers; Bridges and Clouds;
Inner Heart, a Journey; A Split in the Water

FREE e-books
Abstrusion; Wonderland; Fract & Flect;
Year of Divine Madness; 60 Haiku;
Midnight Shootout; Naked Leavings
The Rising; CJ Poetry & Paintings;

www.ebooks.net/poetry/Abstrusion

https://www.everand.com/author/572119332/Candice-James

10 PAK — 5

THE LONG POEMS

by
Candice James

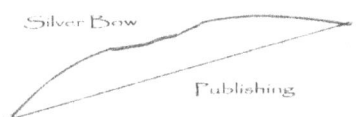

720 – 6th Street, Box # 5
New Westminster, BC
V3C 3C5   CANADA

Title: 10 PAK -5 The Long Poems
Author: Candice James
Copyright © 2025 Silver Bow Publishing
Cover Painting: "Icy Blue" painting by Candice James
Layout/Design: Candice James
ISBN: 9781774033937 (print)
ISBN: 9781774033944 (ebk)j

All rights reserved including the right to reproduce or translate this book or any portions thereof, in any form except for the use of short passages for review purposes, no part of this book may be reproduced, in part or in whole, or transmitted in any form or by any means, electronically or mechanically, including photocopying, recording, or any information or storage retrieval system without prior permission in writing from the publisher or a license from the Canadian Copyright Collective Agency (Access Copyright)
© Silver Bow Publishing 2025

Library and Archives Canada Cataloguing in Publication
Library and Archives Canada Cataloguing in Publication
Title: 10 PAK-5 : the long poems / by Candice James.
Other titles: Ten PAK-five Names: James, Candice, 1948- author. Identifiers: Canadiana (print) 20250310317 | Canadiana (ebook) 20250311666 | ISBN 9781774033937 (softcover) | ISBN 9781774033944 (Kindle) Subjects: LCGFT: Poetry. Classification: LCC PS8569.A429 A6125 2025 | DDC C811/.54—dc23

FOREWORD

The poems in this book are long poems set out in such a way as to allow the reader to rest on each page to fully digest the meaning and let their imagination run free to see the visuals and images the words are painting.

This layout gives the reader the best of experiences as they go through the poems and pages.

CONTENTS

DESTINED DREAMS / 9

AD INFINITUM — DE PROFUNDIS / 33

BYGONE DAYS / 51

DEAD OR ALIVE / 69

THE BUTTERFLIES KNOW MY NAME / 87

DIMENSIONALIZING / 99

AFTERMATH OF THE FLAMES / 121

THE MOON LOST ITS SHINE / 139

THE THROWING / 149

MILKY WAY STARDUST / 157

Author Profile / 167

Destined Dreams

I stood inside my dream
asleep, awake and aware,
watching the dawn expand
into yellow, orange and gold;
and then raindrops fell
into the depth of my desire
and danced with the heat
of a yesterday breeze
painting old memories alive
in a shimmering rainbow
of destined dreams.

All day I rested in the arms
of oblivion's Pseudo Nirvana
until the twinkle of stars,
riding a sparkling trail of dust,
broke through my reverie
and awakened my dream
from its beautiful sleep
and immersed it gently
into a mystical moment.

There is something familiar
in this strange magic
I have entered.
Something unknown
yet known.

In the blonde strand
of a pulsating moment
I see your hazy ghost,
misting in and out,
standing in the shadow
of my long-lost forgotten smile.

Seagulls and pristine doves
are clumping together
then breaking apart
brightening and whitening
the cloudless blue sky
painting the watercolor ocean
a pale turquoise, mint-green
with cream tinted waves
cresting and falling ...
cresting and falling ....

I am a small blip
on a small ocean wave.
a disappearing white dot
in the sky pulsating
on and off ... off and on
then vanishing into the blue
to become more than I am:

Cresting and falling.

Cresting and falling
then rising again.

A whiter shade of pale.
A blacker shade of dark.

Dharma's karma.
Karma's dharma.

One the other.

Less or more.
More or less.

I walk the shallows
of an ever-changing shoreline
that once colored
the days of my life,
the days of my childhood,
the days of my mother.

The days
I wish could begin again
and be viewed
through the kaleidoscope vision
of the yesterdays
I carelessly squandered.

Under a marauding scarlet sky,
I see a star bleeding purple
    and spilling
through the vibrating ether.

A spark of blue
slices through the visual
creating new worlds
for my soul to discover.

       So many
         and
       so inviting.

Time seemed to stand tip-toed
on the razor's edge
of heaven's second-hand
weighing itself down
with a collection of tears
it had failed to redeem.

I closed my weary eyes.

I saw the dog I lost
so many years ago
— along with my childhood —
approaching from
a far and distant horizon.

A horizon I recognized...
as my true north.
My true home.

I had been gone so long
living in a state of
ignominious absence.

As I reached out to my dog
I saw him in radiated light.

The centuries had been kind to him.

Not so to me,
but still, he recognized me
and clung to my ghost.

The sky cracked open.
a new sun hung high in the sky
and then of a sudden
the world was a sandbox.

A glorious, elevated
and suspended,
glittering sandbox.

I saw castles
> become skyscrapers
> then sink in the ocean.

I saw tides coming full
> then fleeing the shore.

And all the while
in my little world
I kept building and rebuilding
the indistinct nothingness
of my vapid atmosphere
that was born to die.

I was building sandcastles,
small childish sandcastles,
that continuously crumbled
and rose haphazardly
like wounded phoenixes.

The smoke and flames
charred and burned
then ebbed and died
in the cold clutch
of dying thought patterns
trapped in forever's fist.

For one simple moment in eternity
    it was such a warm feeling
as yesterday held hands with today
then stepped into tomorrow's embrace.

I stood outside myself
asleep, awake and aware
   in the catch
of yesterday's breeze
 and the shimmer
of destined dreams.

Newborn and dying.
Alive and dead.
Here and there.

**AD INFINITUM
DE PROFUNDIS**

I stepped up
onto a velvet skyfall
of satin silky pathways
and walked into
the golden corridor
of my sleeping mind.

The attic hatch was open
so, I swung the ladder down
    and scaled it
into the dimly lit atmosphere.

Dust swirled and danced
in a singular ray of sunlight.

Centered in that ray of light
I saw a silver-edged photo album
by God, himself, designed.

The pages came alive.
There were so many photos,
so many faces and places.

Some I recognized
but, search as I may,
I could not find a likeness of you.

Then over in the alcove,
hidden near the corner of the room,
I thought I heard you whispering.

Then, your whispers began
to slowly become audible
and I heard you singing
      a love song ...
but your lips were not moving.

I closed my eyes
then opened the again.

I saw a rogue wave swallow
a pebbled pristine beach.

I saw the sky pleat and fold
into a corduroy pattern.

I saw the North Star
     spin around
to greet Orion's daughter.

I saw a chunk of coal
become a burning ember,
then turn to sparks
and gleam white-hot.

At the east end of heaven's gate
I saw a haloed glowing angel
astride a pure white Pegasus.

And all the while Heaven's clock
slowly ticked the time away
and nestled in God's shadow
'til the stars came out to play.

Time is the melody
that allows the heart to dance
passing through the glances
of destiny and chance.

Some choose
to skip the dance
and never suspect
what they have missed.

Some choose
to skip the embrace
and never know
the true depth of the kiss.

A flick of the wrist
or an errant twist
can turn a king's satin tunic
to a beggar's threadbare rags.

An errant twist or flick of the wrist
can turn a pauper's slouch hat
to a king's jewel encrusted crown.

On this side of the one-way mirror
we know not what we will become.

Will the dance be slow and soothing:
        a gentle waltz?

or a ribald flurry of flying feet:
    a highland sword dance?

Life passes by like a blurry scene
and then the dance
and the dream are gone.

But time never ceases to pass
over shoreline upon shoreline
     — ad infinitum
     — de profundis

and always ... always
it goes on and on and on —
    until it doesn't.

I am the sun swinging low
on the sky's wrist.
A shiny bangle dusting the horizon,

I am ultimately
a harvest moon
skulking in the shadows,
waiting patiently
for its day in the sun.

A cavalcade of hazy images
warm the frost etched onto my soul:

I am summer beaches
and wave-carved sandbars.

I am midnight bonfires
and yesterday lovers.

BYGONE DAYS

Metaphors, similes, semi-colons.
Exclamation marks, quotations.
Camouflaged poetic rhyme
and unpunctuated sentences
spar with the strands of my thoughts;
and the ink strains pulsate and throb
to coax the pale ghosts
that cohabit this body with me
to come out of hiding
and show themselves.

These pale ghosts
sometimes put on make-up
and masquerade as living beings.

Other times they are bizarre,
donning grotesque masks,
and cackling in high pitched voices.

And sometimes they just relax
and continue to be —
my uninvited audience.

Sometimes a face in a crowd
hazes into my atmosphere
and coaxes temptation
out of hiding.

Chiding, and biding pale ghost its time
it pricks and prods at my senses
until I am transformed
into another myself
but different for the moment.

Sometimes a fleeting feeling.
Sometimes a small crime.

Sometimes
a cold kiss
smacks reality awake.

Sometimes I am the hunter.
Sometimes I am the prey.
But always I am
the unforgiven wanderer
who fell from the bloodless womb
of a soiled, fallen angel.

I am walking through
a forest alive with
a deadly splash of green
where autumn leaves
are wrapped in winter's embrace
inside the deep cold kiss
of a bastardized snowflake.

I am flowing beneath
a sky alive with
a killing slice of purple
where wounded seagulls
defy the call of the sea
and strive to fly
higher and higher and higher
toward the beckoning live wire
and electrocution's vibrant touch
promising a cinematic demise.

I close my weary eyes
and move into the prayer
I am reciting.

I am a rusty knife pleading for
a slick, silver, shiny blade.

I am a tarnished golden goblet
beseeching the powers that be
for a polish of shimmering sheen.

I am a sinner begging redemption.

Twilight is calling my name
and leading me to my reckoning
and midnight is a deepening black
beckoning me into
the dark baptismal basin.

Inside the narrow wood
of pine trees, poplars and birch,
I weave my way through
the scratch and scarce
of scattered branches and bark.

The smell of a winter storm gathering
at the edges of the forest chills me
and I think on days gone by.

There are blurred ghosts
hazing in the narrow woods
slicing through my eyes,
whispering in my ears.

And there are echoes
from ages past
still living and breathing
in this space I call my own.

Here I walk, one last time,
beneath the sun, moon, stars and sky,
as the tender arms of the final winter
gather me into the scratch and scarce
of their haunting magnetic embrace.

then they lay me down to rest,
forever,
in the warmth
of all my bygone days ...
all my days gone by.

DEAD OR ALIVE

I am lost in a carnival
of the undead,
unable to find solace
in my heart or my head.

I'm dazed and confused
in this circle of squares.
I'm lost in this maze
of crumbling stairs.

A white band of skin on my finger
is evidence of a past love gone by

        And sometimes I cry
        but I know not why.

Broken lyrics
loom large in my head.

        Are these lost words?

        Or just words left unsaid.

Is it rain from the sky?
A tear in my eye?

Or a total breakdown instead.

    Try as I may
    I cannot escape
this ghostly carnival of the undead.

The distant echo
of the train whistle haunts me
down to the bones of my soul.

I gather with the hazy shadows
of all my yesterday ghosts
to ride the rails of my mind
down to the soul of my bones.

When the gathering meets the deep
I can fill my basket of need
with baubles, bangles
and one single bead —
and all the things I'll never need.

I am the pale ghost of night
flowing through cobblestone streets
unnoticed by the lovers
hiding in doorways
and under the bridges of time.

I pass by pastoral gardens
I have become one
with a sky without borders
closing in on my fading shadow,
absorbing my ethereal essence.

The faraway echoes
of a timeless universe
pull at my hazy figure
      as I drift
        above
the cobblestone streets

    not certain
if I am dead or alive,

   but certain that
        I am.

A monochromatic tinge
crept in on little mouse feet:
noiseless, innocuous,
on the slick sweat of death's breath
and made my days nondescript.

I've walked through my shadow
        long, long ago
and traded places with a lesser me
that stole all my cherished songs
        and left me empty:
           without music,
           without harmony,
           without rhythm
in a house of mirrored silence.

And now,

the last remnants of color
are fade, fade, fading away
as the monochrome turns to gray
        then black
          then nothing.

And the mice
and small critters slide away
noiseless and innocuous
on the slick, cloyed sweat
of death's breath.

*In this place,
where dead is alive
and alive is dead*

    your eyes
are disembodied sparks
burning the chaff off the dark edge
    of this endless night
      I am walking through.

I am tangled up
In a timeless tango
of motionless motion,
silent sound
and disembodied sparks
exposing the shadow
of your ghost.

> *This is the place*
> *where dead is alive*
> *and alive is dead.*
>
> *This is where I reside.*

THE BUTTERFLIES KNOW MY NAME

Words pass between us
and as soon as they are spoken
they dissolve.

I move closer to the mirror.
My face looks slightly familiar,
like someone I used to know.

I try to go outside myself
to feel where I've come from
and where I'm travelling to.

I search the shifting patchwork sky
for a brighter shade of this blue
    I'm walking through.

Fingers of uncertainty
are strangling the blue,
blurring it to gray
brushed onto the back
of the looking glass
I'm looking into.

And now my face looks unfamiliar
and I can't find
the road I must travel
to come back into myself.

And all my bridges
have washed away.

And the mirror
is dissolving.

Through a rainbow lens
of possibilities,
I search each prism
and color
for the dream I created
so long ago
in the ether of another time,
another place.

Somewhere
there are flowers, pools,
birds and butterflies
that know the pathway
leading to this dream I created
      so long ago.

The flowers won't talk.
The pools remain silent.
The birds speak
an unknown language.

But the butterflies ...
the butterflies know my name.

They whisper the way
        and wipe the lens
        with the flutter of their wings.

I dive into the lens,
through the prisms,
        melt into the colours
and become the dream once again.

The dream I have always been.
        The dream I am.

The butterflies
know my name.

They've always
known my name.

DIMENSIONALIZING

Night rubs its whiskers
against my heart
chafing the edge of emotions
still red and raw at the core.
Dead on the surface.

The wind cracks her knuckles gently
against the streaked window-pane
and I am lost to the world again.

A snowflake in summer.
Liquid lightening.
There for a moment.
Fading like quicksilver
into a stir of echoes.

Vibrating.
Dimensionalizing.

And I am lost to the world
        again.

Painted rain, fingerprint stains
across a dark sky
are random yet repetitive.
Forgotten yet familiar.

> I search them frantically.
> for the key to me.
> The key to set me free
> to be
> more there than here.

I drift away
on the breath of the breeze
and I am lost to the world again ...

... lost to the world again.

I turn memories on and off
in cinematic film clips.

I see the fog of exhaled breath
where there is only empty space.

I stand on the lowest riser
of a cracked and waterlogged staircase
    and I swear
a ghost is standing there,
    watching me
through diamond kaleidoscope eyes.

I turn away
from the summer in that gaze
and the autumn moonglow
hiding in its maze
and re-enter the winter
of a thousand windblown days.

I rise, a pale ghost
lost in a distant eternity
where hedges
and roses intermingle
in a rhapsody
of blended splendor.

An afternoon daydream
abandoned on childhood's doorstep
manifests obliquely
then turns to silver frost
and then the daydream
turns to gold
and puts the stars
back in my eyes.

Sunlight begins to weave
through the weary threads of the dark
chasing it into a distant corner
banned form the cinemascope
film of this day of days.

Standing inside my shadow,
I peer out into a world
that doesn't see me.
Cloaked in my many masks,
I've lost myself too.

Disguised as a ghostly dream,
I am disappearing smoke.
Exhaled, inhaled.
Part of the world yet separate
in my ghostly guise.

This shadowland I wander in
is ragged at the edges,
sore to the touch
and cold as ice.

I cling to my masks
and my loneliness
inside this world of shadows.

Nobody can reach me.

I am the smoky dream
thinning at the edges
dissolving into the atmosphere ...
       soon to be
forever lost to the world.

The sun is a dying flamingo
crashing into the distant horizon
and I am slowly coming alive
inside this dream I have died in.
.

I move deep
into the waters of time
to rock in the roll of the ocean
and rest in the arms of the angels
that have always been
calling me home.

I balance
on the snowy edge
of my thoughts
and call out
to the pale blue tree
that sways against
my ice-pocked heart.

But there is nothing to hold onto.
Not even a forgotten wish.

I float through the haze
of my non-existent days,
a slick liquid satin
on the waters of life
reflecting the rainfall and tears
of days gone by.

I am gleaming
and singing songs

        to the sun and the sea
            ... and
          the dead.

I lift up my eyes
to the stars overhead

and enter

the door of the dead.

Aftermath Of The Flames

In the aftermath of the flames
this mountain shimmers pearl.

The sun dawns
pale ochre jelly slices
of a lucid dream,
deftly avalanched between
cascading shades
of the firmament.

A prayer book
encapsulated by icicles
and sandstone flecks
cries out to wayward angels
and ragged vagrant doves.

Where are
the brave keepers of souls
that have ruled
since time immemorial?

Once all the stars in the sky
had a pattern and trail to trod
and a satchel of never-ending blood
to fill rivers of being that never run dry.
Keeping cycles of birth and death
forever encased in the circle of time.

Times and tides
are ever-recurring
with only slight variations.

Black specks on white tar paper
stand at attention to welcome
ball peened hammers and nails
to make them bleed
    into a new birth
of something other than itself.

On the other side of the page
a glorious steed champs at the bit.

I am the aging equestrian
riding between the dissolving lines
jockeying for perfect position
between the black and white.

My shiny leather boots
are carving new horizons
splashed with blood and words.

The cold steel bullets of reprisal
snarl and bite through the breeze
and drive me perilously toward
the pearl mountain's gaping maw
that's slowly turning to lapis
and blending into the dark night
obliterating the jellied sun
with swords of devastating drool
falling from the tobacco lips
of this dying ludic dream
that's turning to ash.

The aftermath of the flames
that burned my heart to death.
are now only chunks and bits
of crumbled cold charcoal.

All extant wisdom is buried
by an unexpected snowslide
at the base of an errant prayer
lodged in a seam
of this endless night
I keep travelling through.

There is no escape.

I am lost to the world and heaven
and my recorded words and music
are scattered to the winds of never
and will be read and heard no more.

Death rises vainglorious
in surreptitious disguise,
from a grey cloud of mist
turning me inside out
and outside-in
again and again
until I am no longer myself.

For centuries I've exchanged bodies
borne new flesh and bone
to lodge my weary spirit in:
Trying to recall my other selves.
Trying to absolve them of sin.
Laying them in a casket of tin.

But there's nowhere to end
and nowhere to begin.

I see myself in past images:
A poet, an artist, a musician,
an interloping architect.
A renegade, a destroyer,
a warlord and executioner.

Every time I die,
it seems I die too easily.
There is no fear of the dark
as the fire in my soul ebbs
to invisible then to naught.

I always see the same old light;
the same old ghost at the gate.

Guard of the undead souls
the day of the dead has arrived
and I am seeking entry
that I may be dispatched again
into the living mud and clay
of the revolving earth.

That I may live and breathe again
in the realm of flesh and bone
in the aftermath of the flames.

THE MOON LOST ITS SHINE

The pejorative implication
of love's illusory manifestation
is a flaw in the seeking ego.

Into the false innocence
and the blue steel
of your lying eyes
love rages against
a growling, howling wind.

The wailing whisper
of your invocations
are relentless.

I am blinded by
the flickering light
of your wavering eyes.

This dream is not mine.
You are a stranger to me now
and the moon lost its shine
to the uneven siren call
of an errant passing star.

Standing, stranded at your gate
I am trapped in this nightmare.
I am absent in my presence
and you cannot see me
through the dulled stardust.

My words try to scream
but they're trapped
in this dream.

And all that I seem
is that which I am not.

The moon smiles at me,
cradles me close,
kisses my slackened lips,
draws me into its dark
at the far end of
the visible fading light.

I am surrounded by
unending high cement walls
that shout me down
each time I feebly attempt
to climb them.

I left my courage
at the door of love's illusion.
I left my heart
in the depth of its footprint.

I am dust on the doorstep.
I am rust on the iron cross.
I am tin infused with gold.

I am a quartz-diamond.
A worthless gem
of great worth.

I am the lost hope
of a dying dream.

An invalid sequestered
in the locked vault
of a disavowing ego
adrift on sorrow's sea.

Lost on the lost highway
all I can see are
crumbling roadsides
washed away pavement
and looming dead-ends
in front, behind and
on all sides of me.

I always was a stranger to you
and a stranger to myself.

       And,
the moon lost its shine
to the uneven siren call
of an errant passing star
just as I caught a glimpse of it
as it momentarily rose in the sky
and then died in my eyes
           forever.

THE THROWING

So many lingering
long hot summer images,
indelibly imprinted
on my carbon paper mind,
are everlastingly embossed
on gold-leaf pages of my heart.

The shallows of the shore
laugh and sing old songs
and I am mesmerized ...
mesmerized and wanting.

Awake and asleep
in dreams and in reveries
I've longed for these summers
of the long ago past:
      In the mornings
calling out to the rising sun.
      In the evenings
wishing on a shooting star.

Ah, but I can't
strike a matchstick
and light the ocean on fire
and I can't polish
and shine a rogue wave
surfing a lost yesterday tide
in the dreamland
I always return to.

I throw wishes to the sky
that has lost its raindrops.
I throw droplets of light
to the dusk that has lost its way.
I throw new hopes and dreams
to the bereft and broken hearted.

I throw your memory into the fire.

As I turn the stone-cold handle
on the door of impending death
I watch your memory burn to ash
in the all-consuming heat
of the throwing.

Milky Way Stardust

Milky Way stardust
spills softly into my mind
and I am swept away
into a world of chance,
of change, of free range
and slow powerful dance.

A red rowboat on the right.
A blue skiff on the left
and a runabout on the lake.

A canoe at the water's edge
and a kayak unattended,
at rest on the shore.

Ocean waves and stardust
mix an elixir of raw energy.
A tower of power
pinnacling the tree of life
beside the waterlogged log
of destiny's drowning.

Demise is no surprise
in this land of swaying lockets
that once belonged to me
and now hang sparkling
and shimmering evanescent
around a lost dove's neck.

I walk the shallows
of an old familiar ocean
and count the tidal pools
as the gulls glide overhead
careening and keening
as I pull old memories
from my treasure chest
of precious moments.

I close my eyes.
In the distance
I see a barefoot child
building sandcastles
on a lonely stretch of beach
nestled tightly into the corner
of this dimly lit desolate day.

The Milky Way's
ebbing stardust
flows gently from my mind
into the never-ending rivers
of a diamond-studded night
as the dance of romance ends
in the bliss of a wet,
lingering kiss.

AUTHOR PROFILE

Candice James is a professional poet, musician, singer, songwriter and visual artist. She was appointed Poet Laureate Emerita of New Westminster BC by order if City Council in November 2016 after serving 2 back-to-back three-year terms as Poet Laureate. She is founder of Royal City Literary Arts Society, and Fred Cogswell Award for Excellence in Poetry and past president of the Federation of BC Writers. She's a full member of the League of Canadian Poets and the author of 31 books of poetry through 6 Publishing Houses.

Her first book A SPLIT IN THE WATER was published in 1979 by Fiddlehead Poetry Books, University of New Brunswick CANADA. Her awards include Pandora's Collective Citizen of the Year; and Bernie Legge Platinum Awards Artist of the Year.